CV

◄ *Three Sunflowers*, acrylic on canvas

kim parker
HOME
A LIFE IN DESIGN

Stewart, Tabori & Chang, New York

Published in 2008 by Stewart, Tabori & Chang
An imprint of Harry N. Abrams, Inc.

Library of Congress Cataloging-in-Publication Data:
Parker, Kim.
Kim Parker home / photographs by Albert Vecerka.
p. cm.
Includes bibliographical references and index.
ISBN-13: 978-1-58479-664-0 (alk. paper)
ISBN-10: 1-58479-664-2 (alk. paper)
1. Parker, Kim—Themes, motives. 2. Interior decoration—United States.
3. Design—United States. I. Vecerka, Albert. II. Title.
NK2004.3.P39K56 2008
747—dc22
2007027457

Editor: Dervla Kelly
Designer: Anna Christian
Production Manager: Jacquie Poirier

The text of this book was composed in Miller
Printed and bound in China

10 9 8 7 6 5 4 3 2

HNA
harry n. abrams, inc.
a subsidiary of La Martinière Groupe

115 West 18th Street
New York, NY 10011
www.hnabooks.com

To my husband Felipe,

to my family, to Gil, to furry angels Maggie and Wendy,

and a precious bouquet of friends—for their love,

wisdom, and generosity of spirit.

contents

Foreword   8

Preface   10

Overture   12

Following Dreams   24

Fashion Years   38

Urban Inspirations   58

Interiors   86

Accents   102

Dinnerware   116

Abstract Gardens   128

Design Philosophy   150

Resources   158

foreword

I first met Kim many years ago in Brazil at a music festival. We quickly became friends the way one becomes friends in Brazil. But our encounter evolved into a deeper friendship at a time when we were both trying to find our way in the world. In New York we played a recital together, Kim with her flute and I at the piano. It was a difficult program of Mozart, Prokofiev, and Copland. I remember the beauty of her sound and the sensitivity of her phrasing. It was easy to play with her. Preparing for that program was a joyous process full of musical insights and discoveries. I started to understand the intuitive aspect of Kim's talent, but I was not yet able to fully comprehend its depth.

For a while we lost touch with each other. When we next met, Kim had become a successful artist, painter, and textile designer. The textile designs she showed me were so abundant and beautiful that I just looked in awe at her work. The music she creates with her art is powerful and intense, her use of color like harmony in music. Her shapes and structures, whether in flowers or abstract compositions, have a rhythmic logic and vitality. It was then that I saw how unerring her intuition was, to what depths it could take her, and I started to rethink my own creative processes. Often I would go to an exhibit of the Great Masters and leave with such a desire to create with my own hands and mind—Kim's work has that same power for me. The colors in her paintings inspire me to create colors at the keyboard with sounds. I recently went to a Matisse exhibit. As I was looking at a painting of the south of France done in yellows and blues, I was struck by the similarities between the worlds Kim and Matisse inhabit on canvas. Matisse said that if you want to become a painter, you should cut out your tongue so that you would only be able to speak with a brush. I believe this quality emerges in Kim's work. She possesses a refined intuition, a generous heart, and an unerring talent to absorb and create beauty.

Kim has always been for me an example of a woman who remains true to her gut feelings, someone who is able to sift through input from the outside world. In the difficult world of fashion I saw Kim, despite many obstacles, make a name for herself based upon her pure vision. Ultimately, success is being able to supply our own hearts with some measure of pleasure and beauty.

Recently I moved from New York to live in Paris. On a rainy afternoon I went looking for a birthday present to send to Kim. I don't have much talent for finding presents so it was a small miracle that I found a beautiful, rare book on painter and textile artist Sonia Delaunay. It was the right book.

I'd like to think that in some way I might have unknowingly contributed to the birth of this book, through which we can share Kim's thoughts, journey with her into her dream, and get a glimpse into her creative process. This book is an invitation for each one of us to open a door and walk toward our own dreams, to make them as real as we are able to. Kim manages to take us gently by the hand and show us how.

Sonia Rubinsky

preface

When I started working on this book, I envisioned pages that would celebrate my love for color, for painting gardens, and for New York City life. As I ran around Manhattan's streets with my camera, taking snapshots of her colorful flea and flower markets, I became aware of what the city meant to me, how excited I still was, even after almost two decades, to be living in her familiar embrace. Almost every street held some kind of memory from which I could chart a colorful, complex journey to the present. Marc Chagall said, "I found my lessons in the city itself, at each step, in everything. I found them among the waiters in cafes, the concierges, peasants, and workers. Around them hovered the astonishing light of freedom which I had seen nowhere else."

It was a challenge for me to select which stories to share from almost three decades of my life—from my rich, early musical past to my career in design. In retelling these experiences, I relived many deeply moving moments as well as some difficult ones, all of which helped shape and define my course and direction as an artist. This book began as yet another garden for me to render. It blossomed into a tapestry larger than anything I had ever attempted with my paintbrushes.

The road to my own label was a most unconventional and circuitous path—a journey that unveiled valuable and difficult life lessons. I believe that where passion, risk, patience, determination, and integrity exist, one's Divine connection cannot be severed.

Wild Roses,
acrylic on canvas

11

Overture

From my childhood into my twenties I pursued a serious career as a classical flutist. Having come from a family of gifted musicians, I never questioned this path. By the time I was eight years old it was clear that I loved playing the flute, and the years of study that followed were rich with musical experiences.

In my teens I spent memorable summers performing in an orchestra in residence at Tanglewood, the summer residence of the Boston Symphony Orchestra, working closely with great musicians and such legendary conductors as Leonard Bernstein. I also performed in master classes with flutist Jean-Pierre Rampal at the 92nd Street Y in New York City. Competitions, concerts, music festivals, teaching, performing in Europe, and graduating from Oberlin Conservatory of Music with a degree in flute performance all seemed to indicate that my life and career were heading toward becoming a professional classical musician.

But between the lines on the sheet music I could be found tucked away someplace with my small box of paints. I remember rainy

Berkshire evenings in my room at Tanglewood when I found refuge
filling books with my hand-painted designs and vivid, floral-patterned
borders. And throughout my childhood, before the flute had even
entered my small hands, my fingers were often stained with Magic
Marker from my hours immersed in drawing.

When asked why I walked away from a promising career as a
classical flutist after so many years of serious study and dedication,
I have never been able to provide a simple answer. Painting always
provided me with a kind of creative expression that placed less emphasis on perfection and offered greater artistic freedom. I could spend
hours deeply immersed in color and design—it came as easily to me
as breathing.

I believe in every artist's life, there is at least one defining moment that stands apart, that leaves an indelible mark and provides an everlasting foundation of validation to launch one's creative journey. One experience that had a most profound emotional effect on me happened when I was sixteen and Leonard Bernstein was in residence at Tanglewood. He had been my hero since I was very little. By the time I was eight, his pictures graced my bulletin board. I used to leap with excitement behind my closed bedroom door while listening to a recording of him conducting Beethoven's Leonore Overture No.3. Bernstein had an exuberance that, in my opinion, no other musician has ever paralleled. He was in love with life and embodied everything that I believed constituted creative genius.

My flute teacher at Tanglewood was Paul Fried, the former co-principal flutist of the Boston Symphony Orchestra. One morning Paul called me and said, "Kim, tomorrow Leonard Bernstein is conducting your orchestra, and the orchestra is going to be playing a piece he just finished composing, his Divertimento for Orchestra. I have assigned you principal flute for this piece in rehearsal tomorrow under his baton." He then invited me to the concert that night where they'd be premiering the piece so I'd have a chance to hear it for the first time.

I was in shock. My dream was coming true. I was about to play for Leonard Bernstein, my hero. I took my teacher up on his invitation and went to hear the premiere of Bernstein's work that evening. I hoped that the flute part would not be something too demanding, as I knew I would not be able to see the part for more than a few minutes prior to rehearsal the next morning.

At the concert I listened carefully to each movement. Suddenly, three-quarters of the way through the piece, there was a lengthy flute solo that opened the third movement. There it was, this shining oasis for the flute alone, in the middle of this symphonic work.

I didn't sleep that night. The notion of having Leonard Bernstein a few feet away from me on a podium conducting his music the next

"Painting always provided me with a kind of creative expression that placed less emphasis on perfection and offered greater artistic freedom."

morning was beyond a dream. If we were playing something from the standard orchestral repertoire—a Brahms or Beethoven, a Tchaikovsky or Mahler symphony—that would have been fine, as I was familiar with those parts. But the next morning our orchestra would be the second orchestra ever to play this new work of his, and there was a flute solo I had never performed. If ever I was going to have to be note perfect, tomorrow was the day.

I had literally fifteen minutes to sit with the flute part prior to rehearsal. I used my time wisely, going directly to the third movement to look over the solo passage. Moments later Bernstein entered the rehearsal hall, full of life and love, energy and joy.

"Good morning," he said ebulliently. "How many of you were at the concert last night?" He paused for a moment, looking over the score, then turned to me and asked, "Flute, what is your name?" to which I replied. "Kim," he said warmly, "I want to start with the flute solo in the third movement. The meter is a bit tricky, but just follow me. I will conduct you through it." And all I remember was that for the first four or five bars of the flute solo, I paid very close attention to his every gesture, following the tempo he had indicated. But after that, I took off on my own, playing through the entire solo passage as if I had known the music my whole life. One note led to the next effortlessly. All fear fell away as I was lifted into what I can only describe as total euphoria musically. I was no longer following his baton but taking flight freely on my own with the beauty of his music.

What I had not noticed while I was playing was that Bernstein had gently stopped conducting me long before, allowing me to continue the solo to the end. And when I finished he came down off the podium, parting a Red Sea of music stands until he reached mine.

"I believe in every artist's life, there is at least one defining moment that stands apart and provides an everlasting foundation of validation to launch one's creative journey."

He took my face in his hands, kissed me, and said, "My dear Kim, you are an artist."

When I look back on this experience, even after so many years, I realize what an emotional milestone it was. It was a defining moment for me as a musician and from that point on I knew that, had I never performed again, I could go to my grave musically fulfilled. Over the years I have come to appreciate more deeply the gift the Universe bestowed on me that summer. Not only had I played for my hero, but also, even more divinely, I had been given the precious opportunity and gift to play his music. This moment provided me with the greatest set of creative wings I could ever have asked for, freeing and permitting me to take artistic flight in any direction.

Following Dreams

After four years of college in a small midwestern town, I craved city rhythms and energies more than ever. I needed to take a break from being a musician. Even with no secretarial skills and no computer knowledge, I somehow managed to find employment in corporate Manhattan. I held jobs at insurance companies, music management agencies and publishing houses, stock brokerages, children's museums, and the United Nations, where I translated French documents.

In the lobby of a tall office building on Lexington Avenue and Fifty-third Street where I was temping hung a vibrant and exuberant Frank Stella sculpture. It was hard to miss this modern art piece when you walked in—it was brilliant with color and wild energy. Each morning when I arrived at work, I gazed up at it for a few minutes before getting in the elevator. Like an injection of oxygen, the colors lifted my spirit. I dreamed of having the life of an artist.

Red Garden, ▶
3 panels,
acrylic on
wood

It wasn't long before I discovered that I could never get used to the cold, stale, fluorescent corporate world, which seemed to me so grey, so devoid of color. Every night after work, I returned home to my small kitchen table in Queens where I sat quietly and painted for hours, immersing myself in my box of paints to restore my inner balance.

But after numerous jobs in the corporate world, I could take no more. The ordinary life I thought I had desired after college lacked color and vitality. So after five years, I left for Europe with my flute in hand, turning my back on my uninspired and colorless existence in Manhattan. I found myself giving concerts in chateaus, teaching and playing chamber recitals in Brussels. Music always seemed to be in the air. The sound of church bells outside my window and the beauty of the landscape were incredible daily sources of joy and inspiration that I never took for granted.

But a year and a half later I returned to New York City. I felt an instant reconnection with her rhythms and a fondness for her familiar streets. I was a bit nervous about returning to live in Manhattan. The musical opportunities were not the same as in Europe. I knew I didn't want to teach the flute anymore, but my only other musical career option was to land a symphony position someplace, and the idea of running around the country taking auditions no longer appealed to me.

While I wasn't sure what was available to me outside of a career in music, I was certain I didn't want to return to the corporate world to earn a living.

One day a family friend, who had seen a book of one hundred textile designs I had put together, suggested I should look for design work in the fashion industry. This was a universe I had absolutely no experience in. Starting over in a whole new creative field seemed to me

like setting the clocks back on my artistic life at least fifteen years, but I decided to give it a try. So, without a degree from the Fashion Institute of Technology or Parsons School of Design, or any experience at all in the industry, I set out to find a job. The only thing I had to show in interviews was a book of original textile designs I had put together over the course of a decade—this book served as my visual resume.

Once I was hired, the landscape changed. I discovered that there was even less freedom of expression in a fashion industry design studio than I ever experienced as a classical musician. My fortes were neither needed nor desired. My freehand approach to painting was not utilized. My color sense, which had gotten my foot in the door in the first place, was ignored and overlooked as well, and I was asked, often by cruel and unforgiving bosses, to re-render existing prints and recolor them according to rigid instructions. I was thrown into an on-the-job education, a kind of boot camp, where I struggled to learn what FIT grads had already conquered technically in school.

No matter how brutal things became during my fashion studio years, I was always grateful to be holding a paintbrush in my hand and to have a paycheck to take home. I knew what it meant to live in a great city like New York and be able to support myself as an artist, even if my self-expression was being severely squelched.

As I had done with my corporate jobs in the past, I would return home at night to undo what had been done to my creative spirit during the day. Even though for eight hours every day I was hired to paint things that were anything but free and expressive, I had not lost my desire to paint. I came home in the evenings with the desire to reconnect with my brush all the more, and continued to fill books with my own designs.

From my time on the job, I gathered an awareness of various market categories—from couture to home design to baby clothes. I was exposed not only to patterns and techniques, styles and color palettes, but also to an entire spectrum of subjects ranging from marketing to fashion, design industry standards to human behavior. In short, I earned my degree from FIT, and a few other degrees along with it.

The first and only formal art classes I had ever taken were at Queens College in New York. It was in this environment that I had been introduced to Color-aid paper. The teacher was a student of the renowned artist and color theorist Josef Albers. The homework assignments—color exercises about juxtaposing form and color to illustrate the complex properties of hues and influences they could have on one another—came naturally to me. My teacher held onto each one of my assignments and told me privately that she thought they were brilliant. "If Albers had seen these, he would have loved them. I want to keep them for future classes if you will allow me."

One of the most painfully memorable jobs I held was for a children's clothing company on Thirty-fourth Street. The stylist who first interviewed me resembled something out of a fairy tale—a caricature of an old witch—as she hovered over my small book of colorful designs, ran her fingers across the surface of each print, then lured me in for employment, as though I were Snow White and she was tempting me with a poisonous apple.

I was hired right away as their resident colorist, which meant that I would be rendering as many color combinations for a given design as I could come up with so the consumer would have several options for a printed garment. On my first day, I was put not in the studio with all the other artists, but in a windowless, airless closet, where two Spanish women sat working shoulder-to-shoulder at sewing machines, sweatshop-style. Apparently there was no other space to put the new kid on the block. There was a large high table and a stool, but no sign of any art supplies.

My boss came into the closet and flashed a small, colorful pair of overalls before me—my first assignment. "See this design I have here? I want you to come up with five to ten color combinations for it," she said. "Have them finished by the end of the day." The pattern was a cheery floral pattern of three colors on a white background, and the assignment seemed like a walk in the park for me. I knew this was going to be easy. I was anxious to get started and prove myself. The only problem was that there were no art supplies. I asked whether the company could provide some paint and brushes and paper, but was told they didn't have the budget. I then suggested that they might supply a box of Color-aid paper, one hundred assorted colorful papers that could be found in any art supply store. I had to have some way to illustrate my

" Even though for eight hours every day I was hired to paint things that were anything but free and expressive, I had not lost my desire to paint.**"**

ideas, and while paper was not a medium I was very comfortable with, the color assortment was rich, so I knew I could create many beautiful combinations for the assignment. My boss agreed, but angrily.

And so I became Henri Matisse, cutting out floral designs with scissors. It was a real challenge to create without a paintbrush, but I swiftly became confident with the medium and mounted fifteen original floral designs in vivid color combinations on small pieces of white cardboard that I had found in packages in the sewing room. Each little floral print sparkled like a small jewel in my memory.

Once I had quite a few of these designs finished, I proudly gathered them and took them in to show my boss. I placed the first design down delicately before her, but she grabbed it off her desk and threw it into her garbage can. Each time I placed one down she tossed it into her garbage, as I looked on in horror. I continued unflinchingly with my presentation until I had no more designs in hand. All my designs were in her trash. " Go back and try again!" she snapped. I looked at my work in her garbage can and asked, "Why didn't you like these?" "I simply don't," she responded. "Go back and try again!"

I left the room shaking. I went back to my closet. I had no idea what I could do to improve upon my presentation. Perhaps Josef Albers would have loved my work, but my boss at a children's clothing company thought it belonged in the trash. I knew I could not produce another design in an environment like that, so soon after I was on to my next job.

Many of the jobs I held in the early days of my design career were similar to the one at the children's clothing company. Studio directors were incapable of understanding and recognizing an artist's feelings and strengths. There were power struggles and ugly displays of envy. There was unnecessary humiliation and abuse. I got fired from my jobs for confronting it, but never regretted losing or leaving a single job. Instead I always felt incredibly lucky to be free of such emotional and artistic constraints.

For a few years, I remained in these fashion studios where I was eventually given more freedom with my brushes and more opportunities to come up with my own designs. Studios started to embrace my ability to quickly establish several marketable color combinations for a design, and handed the technical repainting of the entire design over to someone more technically inclined. I was also asked to create my own designs for children's wear, womenswear, swimwear, and other markets. It all came so naturally to me—this was something I had been doing every night for more than ten years in the privacy of my kitchen. And while it had taken a few years serving as resident colorist in various design studios, I was finally permitted to paint the way I did at home each night, coming up with my own patterns and colorations. I had earned a slice of freedom in an unforgiving industry and for me this was a real victory. I was finally painting in New York City and making a good living.

Fashion Years

After five years, I'd had enough of fashion studio jobs. I felt it was time to take flight with my own designs. I knew this was going to be hard but I was ready to do whatever it took to be successful. There were agents in the city who sold textile designs to the various fashion houses. I contacted a few of them to show them my designs and created a body of original textiles in hopes of being signed on.

Each agency specialized in a particular look or style of art. Some represented artists of computer-generated prints, while others had artists whose work appeared very neat and schooled. Some agencies were strictly silk print houses and weren't interested in selling paper designs; others dealt only with one specific market—whether womenswear, or children's wear. (Today agencies provide designs for all areas of the market.)

One day a fellow painter friend pointed me in the direction of a particular agency he felt would sell my work. This agency represented

many talented textile designers from all over the world. They sold both paper and silk prints, and the head of the agency generously taught me in fifteen minutes how to paint on silk. And like the ballet dancer in the film *The Red Shoes*, my love affair with silk had begun.

Silk was the perfect surface for my textiles. It brought out a rich saturation of color and my designs came to life like never before. I would begin by stretching the silk over a wooden frame. After coating the silk with gutta serti, I painted the design. Then I removed the silk from the frame and steamed it in a tall paper roll in a lobster pot on the stove for two hours to set the colors and make them more brilliant. The next morning I took my designs to the dry cleaner to remove the gutta. This made them soft and irresistibly floppy, the way silk should feel. Then I cut each design into its square or rectangular shape with pinking shears, labeled it on the back, numbered it, logged it in a large book I kept as my design file, photographed it for further documentation, and finally placed it on a sheet of acid-free white paper in my case—like warm cookies—ready to be sold.

I couldn't stop painting. I painted two hundred silk designs a month, submitting them almost daily to my new agent, and before I knew it my sales started rolling in. It was a thrill for me each time one of my designs was bought by a fashion house or market and used in a line. After a few months of successful sales, and with support and advice from my husband, I decided to break free from the agency. With pen and pad in hand, and with two heavy cases of designs, I entered every single building on Broadway and on Seventh Avenue, and jotted down the names of the fashion companies in the directories. I rode up and down elevators, introducing myself and leaving my business card with receptionists and anyone else who would take

one, and asking for the names of the people in charge of purchasing prints. Each night I went over my contacts and prepared to call and follow up with them the next day. In retrospect I cannot believe the kind of energy this took. Many of these companies were dead ends and never bought a print in their lives. Some were curious. Others probably viewed me as a Willy Loman. But this was how I built my Rolodex.

During the years I sold my own prints, I had the good fortune of meeting with and selling to some of the top fashion designers in the industry. One afternoon in Diane von Furstenberg's West Village office, I did my usual displaying for her then head designer Catherine Malandrino. Catherine was familiar with my work—I had sold her a number of my designs for Diane's line. Diane suddenly appeared on the scene, looking over my shoulder while I went through the motions of displaying my silks. "What studio is this?" Diane asked. Catherine replied, "Kim Parker Designs." Catherine then informed Diane that some of my designs were already in her spring collection, and Diane asked which ones. Within moments, Diane disappeared and returned with a skirt from the back room that had my design on it. She handed it to me with a smile and said, "This is for you."

Of course during the many years I sold my silk designs to the fashion industry, I also had unpleasant experiences. One appointment in particular had the magical ending of an O. Henry story, which is why I always enjoy telling it.

A lingerie house on Madison Avenue—notorious print buyers—called on me one day to come in and show my collection of designs. It was my first appointment in their showroom and the owner bought twenty designs from me on the spot. A few months later, they called

" Silk was the perfect surface for my textiles. It brought out a rich saturation of color and my designs came to life like never before. "

me back to see more of my prints. Again I brought my cases over, and again they purchased a few more of my silk prints.

Several months later I received a phone call from one of the designers who purchased the last batch of prints. She told me they'd decided that they didn't want the designs they had bought from me a few months earlier. "We hope that's all right," she said. "Can you come pick them up?" She then asked for a refund. I knew this was not standard protocol with bigger print companies in the design industry and that returning designs months after purchasing them was most unprofessional and unethical. But as I was on my own rather than part of a larger agency, I knew I had to accept the situation gracefully and refund their money as well as retrieve my designs.

When I returned home that night after picking up my designs, I decided to reorganize my silk portfolio for the appointments I had the following day. I was horrified to discover that one of the two prints they had returned had thumbtack holes poked through it and one-third of the silk design was actually missing, cut away by scissors. I wasn't sure whether to confront them or simply overlook it. As was typical of me during my years in sales, I decided not to confront them. I told myself that it was just one print out of hundreds I had in my cases, and that even with the portion that was cut away and the holes that had been poked through it, the print miraculously still looked good enough to sell.

Months later, the same lingerie company called me to schedule another print appointment. I again rolled my cases to their showroom and met with their new team of designers. They all agreed on a particular design and enthusiastically decided to buy it. A private smile came over my face as they had repurchased the print with the holes and one-third of the design missing.

Another memorable appointment was the first time I went to Jill Stuart's showroom off Seventh Avenue. I thought I had entered paradise. Jill was one of my favorite designers. She loved pink as much as I did, and her fashions had a gypsy soul that I couldn't resist but could barely afford. I remember waiting in her showroom while her design team looked through my prints. Surrounded by dreamy organza and velvet garments, I felt like a Renaissance princess.

At the end of the appointment Jill came into the room to look at the selection of prints her team had pulled aside for her to see. "I want to see them all!" she exclaimed with what seemed like an enthusiasm equal to what I felt for her creations. By the end of that first print appointment, she had purchased some of my favorite floral designs and soon after I watched them grace her runway shows and shine like gems on the racks in her SoHo store.

She was extremely generous and told me to select whatever dresses and skirts I wanted from her store. It was a dream come true. I came away with gorgeous velvet skirts and embroidered dresses, and, of course, beautifully made silk garments with my own designs on them. These fashions ended up in movies such as *The Princess Diaries*, made the cover of *Women's Wear Daily*, and were featured in numerous fashion magazines, so it was truly an enchanting opportunity for a few seasons.

> **"**It suddenly dawned on me that my decision to walk away from a musical career had not been futile.**"**

Another appointment with a seventy-year-old fashion studio head, formerly a Parsons School of Design art professor, left quite an impact on me. As I always did, I opened my cases of prints and began displaying them. For almost thirty minutes, he looked at my work without saying a word. This usually indicated that my work did not appeal to the person. But the silence was broken when he asked where I went to school to study art. I told him I went to Oberlin, that I was a music major. "No wonder," he said, smiling. "Your work is extremely lyrical. No art student could ever have produced these. Good thing you never studied art formally—they would have tried to destroy that."

This moment struck a deep chord within me. It suddenly dawned on me that my decision to walk away from a musical career had not been futile, and I started to realize, after this meeting, that the repertoire I had studied and fallen in love with over the years had somehow worked its way into the architecture of my designs.

The Parsons School of Design Printsource Show was an arena I entered into half way through these years of selling my own designs. It was an opportunity for me to set up a booth in a print show, and sell my work. Buyers would come to the show from all over the country for the sole purpose of purchasing textile designs for their collections. So for a few years I participated in Parson's Printsource Show—growing my list of clients, and expanding my market. I started selling to the big department stores such as: Target, Sears, May Company, Marshall Fields, etc. companies I hadn't sold to before.

That was the beginning of my sales to the home decor market. Buyers from Garnet Hill, Pottery Barn, Anthropologie, Martex, Crate & Barrel, all bought my textile designs and saw the vision and potential of bedding and home design in them. The show was a huge success, and we made out brilliantly. Although an exhaustive three days of selling on my feet with my husband, the risk paid off. My markets had broadened considerably, and before long, soft blankets from Anthropologie, Kids bedding from Pottery Barn Kids, sheets and robes from Garnet Hill, were in their catalogues and stores, springing up everywhere.

During the years of selling my designs to many of the top designers in the fashion industry, a number of them encouraged me to start my own label. My confidence was boosted by designers such as Anna Sui, Carolina Herrera, Calvin Klein, Donna Karan, and countless others who employed my prints in their showrooms and collections. I watched as my work was paraded up and down their runways. I saw my designs showcased in advertisements and catalogues. I had decided it was time to launch my own label.

I had spent years canvassing, doing market research, and building my sense of confidence and voice in the industry. In seven years, I had produced seven thousand designs and had seen them perform in everyone else's collections. But during that same period I had also created what my husband lovingly referred to as the "treasure chest"—a suitcase full of my favorite textiles, ones that I refused to part with, ones I most cherished. Perhaps I knew in my heart these would one day be born under my own label.

I launched my label, Kim Parker Home, at the Licensing Show at the Javitz Center in New York. This show allowed artists to decorate

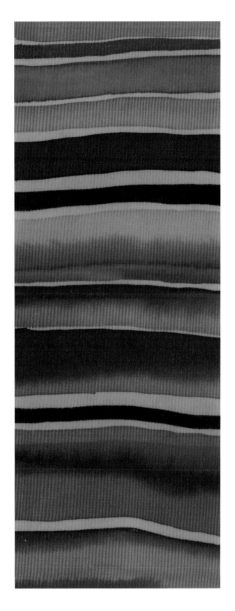

their booths as they wished, to showcase their design capabilities for potential manufacturers. The show produced many fruitful connections from Lenox China and Block China to Editions Limited. An art gallery in the Hamptons offered me a gallery show. Stationery manufacturers and rug companies were interested in signing me on and helping me launch my own label.

To this day, the feeling of wonder and excitement never fades. I am still touched by the birth of a rug, bedding and bath product, fabric, dinner plate, decorative pillow, wall hanging, and sheet of stationery and I sigh with a sense of deep gratitude, knowing full well the distance traveled to this place.

I share these stories because they are all part of the garden of my life as a designer and artist. I believe each story has worked its way into my designs and canvases. And I realize now how tenaciously I held on to my paintbrushes and refused to allow people to change my artistic vision. Many of the jobs I held tried to rip that away from me, to strip my work of its organic nature, but were unsuccessful. And whenever I drive down Lexington Avenue past the office building with the vibrant Stella sculpture in the lobby, tears fill my eyes. I am reminded of a young woman in New York City who followed her dream—and found it.

Urban Inspirations

L iving in a city makes one appreciate even the simplest aspects of nature. It is rare in New York City to be able to connect to nature through a back window, let alone to own a plot of land for gardening. We are fortunate to live in a brownstone apartment that has a green courtyard right outside our living room windows. We deeply cherish it. I have hung feeders to attract finches, jays, cardinals, mourning doves, sparrows, catbirds, and of course pigeons, all of whom come right up to the glass to look in at us. I dream of having my own garden one day, a garden like Monet's Giverny, the painter's sanctuary in France. For now, that kind of floral abundance is what I try to create indoors. Flowers represent joy and life to me and I garden with paint, not soil. Creating an interior garden in a city setting restores me.

◄◄ *Garden of Love,* acrylic on canvas

"In our neighborhood, along Second Avenue, there is a park where a spectacular array of tulips in fruity colors—pale peaches, pinks, deep plums, vibrant yellows, and oranges—appears every spring, and the array of colors seems to get more beautiful each year."

◄ *Beach Garden*, acrylic on canvas

More and more I am aware of the importance of beauty in my life. I often sit quietly in my living room and watch the birds peck at the suet, and feel the good fortune of having a home in a city that I love. Our home is our sanctuary. It is filled with colorful objects to which we have a personal connection. Even the smallest things have great potential to invite sparkle and joy, and I am always amazed at how our nest keeps becoming more beautiful to my eyes.

There is beauty to be found in the city all year round. Central Park is lovely in every season. In the fall the park is as picturesque as any country road I have ever driven down, its sugar maples bursting with glorious oranges, reds, and yellows. In the spring, along the West Side Highway, I am always stunned by the unexpected injections of bright yellow daffodils that grow in large clusters as well as by the many puffy pink blossoms on the cherry trees lining Riverside Park.

"Finding beauty in a city might be a challenge, but I think city life has somehow heightened my appreciation for beauty, enabled me to see beauty in unexpected places, and fueled all the more my desire to create it."

In our neighborhood downtown, along Second Avenue, there is a park where a spectacular array of tulips in fruity colors—pale peaches, pinks, deep plums, vibrant yellows and oranges—appears every spring, and the array of colors seems to grow more beautiful each year.

We love living close to Union Square and the Greenmarket. It is a favorite inspirational location, a yearlong celebration of nature, where farmers and merchants from the Hudson Valley and other local farms come to sell their flowers, produce, and homemade sweets. Buckets of zinnias, dahlias, and roses burst with color. It is always a joy to stroll among the colors and cart home bouquets for the kitchen table.

I also love walking the city streets with my camera and snapping pictures of people's gardens. I never paint from these photos but come away with a tremendous yearning to recapture them somehow on canvas or textile. I am touched by the appreciation for a small, humble plot of land and the efforts to bring as much beauty into that plot as possible. Even window boxes are little treasures, vignettes of beauty, and wonderful sources of inspiration for me.

Throughout this chapter I have included some of the photos I have taken of the city's local flea and flower markets and intimate

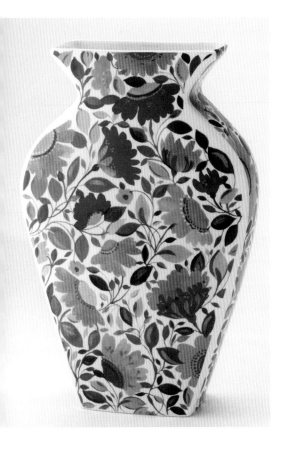

Rose Trellis, ▶▶
acrylic on canvas

garden plots. These are just a few examples, a few precious snap-shots of urban gardens, both community-made and public, that add a feeling of softness to the city's neighborhoods. In our zip code, we are fortunate to have a few of them that surround us. These gardens are injections of joy and connections to the natural world that I don't take for granted.

An artisan friend and glassblower had a small shop on Eliza-beth Street that sadly closed not too long ago. Michael Anchin's shop was another kind of urban garden for me, an oasis where I could lose myself among the most exuberantly colorful glass lamps, vases, and cups, all infused with his passionate breath. Many photographs of his

beautiful handblown glass pieces are strewn throughout this book. His pieces adorn the window ledges, mantel, and coffee table in our home. My husband and I used to make a weekly pilgrimage to his store just to lift our spirits. I now must own close to sixty pieces of his work, all of which inspire me artistically. When the midday sun beams through the anatomies of the pieces along the window ledge in my living room, the room sparkles with healing color.

Finding beauty in a city might be a challenge, but I think city life has somehow heightened my appreciation for beauty, enabled me to see beauty in unexpected places, and fueled all the more my desire to create it. I have always painted with a single mission—to try and create what I felt was beautiful. Beauty is of course subjective. We all see things with different eyes. But flowers have always been a tremendous inspiration to me. To this day, when I paint them,

whether on dinnerware, rugs, decorative pillows, bedding, or canvas, I feel joyful. Through painting I feel empowered to communicate the joy that flowers bring to me. I love the idea that by expressing my love for them on canvas or textile, I can give flowers eternal life.

"Beauty is of course subjective. We all see things with different eyes."

◄ *Ram*, acrylic
on canvas

"New York provides me with inspiration, satisfying my never-ending thirst for connecting to color and finding beauty. Almost every street has some kind of memory, from which I can chart a colorful, complex journey to the present."

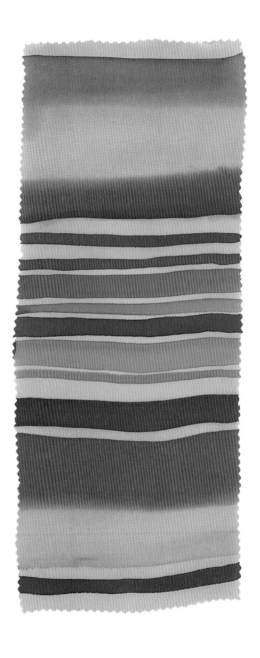

"Flowers represent joy and life to me and I garden with paint, not soil."

"When my husband and I lived in the Catskills, the front of our house faced a huge field of chicory flowers that gave the impression that a beautiful blue sky had fallen on the field."

"There is something about the color yellow that makes me feel even more euphoric when I paint."

"I see patterns, rhythms, and color stories wherever I go. These amazing purple pom poms took me by surprise while on a walk along the Hudson River."

Interiors

When I was a child, I used to curl up with my mother on the couch to look at art books on Matisse, Bonnard, and Vuillard. I was drawn to their incredible use of color and fascinated by their ability to combine dense patterns. Later I'd sit for hours in my bedroom painting bookmarks covered with floral and geometric prints and layering them across the surface of my desk. As I finished each one I felt excitement in seeing them together, a sense of abundance and joy for my eyes.

When I decorate a room and arrange pieces, I try to have an understanding of the dialogue between objects as well as a sensitivity to the balance of color and pattern. Some colors are bold and act as the main theme for the room, while others provide a soft accompaniment. Similarly some patterns are the first thing you notice when you enter a room because their energy or scale catches your eye, while other less noticeable patterns serve as accents.

It is a challenging exercise to combine rich color and varied pattern without making a room appear too busy, but I like this challenge. I want people to walk in and immediately be embraced by the healing power of color.

My designs, with their succulent colors and exuberant energy, present a challenge to someone accustomed to a softer palette or less energetic motif in a room. It's a good idea to pull one of the dominant colors from a fabric, pillow, or painting, and cover a chair or sofa with that solid color. One great solid piece of furniture can really stabilize a room and act as the perfect accompaniment to color-rich rugs, pillows, and fabrics. In our living room our "troika couch" performs this function. I found it at the flea market one day in perfect condition, and fell in love with its graceful, rolled arms and Victorian curves. It has proven itself the perfect backdrop to my rugs and

pillows with its rich red velvet color that, touchingly, has become more iridescent with time.

One of my favorite things to do on weekends is to go to the flea market. The Chelsea Flea Market in New York is one of the few such pleasures left in the city, but sadly it is fighting for its life as the lots it occupies are swiftly being taken over by skyscrapers. For more than a decade and a half I have been combing these lots and finding treasures. My husband and I have become regulars and have developed relationships with the vendors over the years.

Part of what appeals to me is finding objects from totally different eras and cultures and bringing them together in a room. I have brought home Haitian paintings, African iron sculptures and sweetgrass throws, Turkish mosaic tables, Mid-Century modern lamps, and Victorian loveseats, chairs, and cabinets. I have collected English and Bavarian cups and saucers, Chinese parrot sculptures and vases, and hand-painted fabrics from India. Our home is filled with these treasures that all seem to coexist nicely.

I have a particular fetish for chairs and not enough space for all of the ones I have collected over the years. Chairs are such wonderful canvases for me. Their anatomies are the perfect models for my upholstery fabrics and pillows. When I see one with a good frame, I cannot resist bringing it home for a fitting with one of my fabrics. Many of the pieces we have carted home were not in great shape and needed major help, but reupholstering them and bringing them back to life with my fabrics makes me feel more emotionally invested in these pieces.

I never shop in department stores for new furniture because to me newly made pieces lack life. I am attracted to old-world craftsmanship, to unique pieces that cannot be found any longer. I like the idea

> **"**Part of what appeals to me is finding objects from totally different eras and cultures and bringing them together in a room.**"**

that a chair has remained classic and strong over time. The evidence of life and age in anything gives it greater charm and deeper appeal.

Flea markets are about nostalgia. They reignite old love affairs with objects from our childhoods, keeping us connected to the past and its craftsmanship. They can trigger creativity and inspire in unexpected ways. I have purchased art books that have stirred my desire to go home and paint or write, as well as vintage pieces of clothing that triggered ideas for my own designs. I go there with others in mind as I browse, finding vintage opera recordings for my father, any beautiful green object for my mother, or quirky oddities that my brother, who invents clever sculptures, could employ in his work.

Somehow the ritual of these weekend visits never gets stale. You never know what you are going to find and that element of mystery keeps the hunt fresh. The flea market is a wonderland of the unexpected, a place to lose oneself and encounter a meaningful variety of treasures that speak to the heart and refresh both space and spirit.

One Sunday in January, in the freezing rain, we came across a Victorian loveseat at our favorite haunt, the Chelsea Flea Market. The springs were popping out and the upholstery was moldy. I stood there with my husband debating how I would give it a makeover, wondering which fabric design of mine might bring it back to life and knock a few decades off its saddened frame. I had always wanted a Victorian

"In the bedroom I have tried to create another kind of garden with a lighter color palette of pinks and sage greens and white—gentle colors to wake up to."

loveseat. All things Victorian appeal to me and our living room was filled with other such elegant ladies to whom I have given facelifts with my fabrics. This particular loveseat with its oval center really captured my heart and the investment and commitment to its transformation, I admit, scared me a bit. I wondered whether, after all was said and done, I would be happy with the end result. After about thirty minutes of questioning whether I was inviting an unwanted guest into our home, I finally committed and hauled it home in our car.

An editor from the *London Guardian* had seen a glimpse of my remodeled loveseat in an article *Elle Decoration* had run a few months prior, and called to see whether they could run a feature on our home's interior. The writer was told to include this loveseat in the story and the photographer was given specific instructions to photograph the loveseat with nothing else around it. In short, it made the cover of the magazine section. This seemed incredible to me at first, but once the issue came out I gained real confidence in the makeover. There she was, a cover girl.

Another solid piece of furniture in our living room is a Victorian armchair that I recently upholstered in an apple-green velvet. I use this color in just about every design I have ever painted, and I love how the armchair pulls that same color from my Bolero rug. These solid pieces offer the eye a place to rest, and enhance and celebrate the rich colors in my patterns.

In the bedroom I have tried to create another kind of garden with a lighter color palette of pinks and sage greens and white—gentle colors to wake up to. Our bedroom has a bit of a romantic quality to it, with vintage lamps that cast a warm, yellow glow and mirrors that reflect the colors in the paintings and patterned bedspread.

"Flea markets are about nostalgia. They reignite old love affairs with objects from our childhood, keeping us connected to the past and its craftsmanship.**"**

Here again I have flea market finds from different places: an old white antique dresser my mother found for me; a bureau from a secondhand furniture store in the city; and a small mosaic night table I found in the Catskills. The tops of dressers and night tables are perfect stages for high-impact or delicate arrangements of objects and I love to create vignettes in these spaces. It's just as much fun combining smaller pieces as it is arranging larger ones in a room. I use dainty English floral saucers to hold jewelry, and place all types of decorative mirrors both lying down on flat surfaces or upright on the dresser to bounce light and color around the room. I am a collector of vintage mirrors and I enjoy hanging them because they open up a room and bring in more light. In Manhattan apartments they are useful tools for creating the illusion of more square footage. I also love hanging mirrors across from one another on opposite walls so they reflect fragments of paintings and other colorful objects in the room, bringing a romantic dimension to the room.

My bedding collections, like my rugs, contain rich colors and dense floral patterns. When I lived in Europe I remember driving past a field of the most glorious poppies. I immediately pulled my car over to the side of the road and ran right for them, falling backwards into them with the most incredible sense of floral bliss! This memory has never left me, and when I design for bedding, I try to re-create that same energy and feeling of bucolic abundance.

Our headboard was a gift from my mother, who had been using it over a bureau for years. It's one of those delicate vintage mirrors whose white wooden frame is partially chipped from age. It doesn't bother me when something is slightly chipped or peeling because its age endears it to me all the more. Unlike most headboards, it doesn't eat up a lot of space in our bedroom but rather brings space in, as it reflects the light from the front windows.

Smaller pieces like the metal magazine rack and the footstools that I've reupholstered are fun additional accents. They tuck away easily and are functional as well as decorative. I enjoy finding these types of pieces at flea markets because they too can add colorful impact and can brighten a room.

Occasionally, either with the change of season or simply based on my mood, I rotate my quilts, rugs, duvets, and canvases. Every room is a blank canvas for me, and inventing new dialogues between pieces and mixing furniture from different periods within a given space keeps our home ever changing and dynamic. It is an exciting challenge to make various pieces come together with humor, or harmony, or even a bit of tension—but just the right degree of it—so that the end result conveys a positive, uplifting feeling.

Accents

When it comes to decorating, my main objective is to create a space that feels embracing and positive. I know what I respond to and what feels good to me. Rich exuberant color and energetic, bold pattern are key aspects in my design aesthetic. There is a trend these days for minimalism that I see in many of the magazines—a wash of white, black, and beige. I understand this quiet, minimal approach, but frankly, if I had to come home every day to such a bland palette, it would put me to sleep.

Color is like a vitamin for me. A bright, succulent red begonia plant on the kitchen table awakens my spirit and infuses it with energy. I can feel that same lift with a richly colored decorative pillow, rug, bedspread, dinner plate, upholstered chair, vase, or shower curtain!

For those less likely to fill a space with as much pattern and color as I do, or for those who might opt for a softer, safer color scheme like beiges or whites, I would suggest experimenting with bold color in something smaller, like one dynamic decorative pillow, to start. Place it on the couch and see if it makes you feel good.

One of my great pleasures in decorating a room is in adding colorful accents. This could mean a colorful pillow, a footstool, a brightly colored glass vase, a painting, or a throw draped over the arm of a couch. Covering a smaller piece like a hassock with a bold and energetic pattern can also add color and life to a room. For those less inclined to use as much print as I do in a space, this is a good way to introduce a bit of playfulness and movement.

At flea markets I always look for hassocks because they are easy to cover with fabric. They vary slightly in shape and size and are actually quite useful. They tuck away nicely under chairs and tables and can be brought out when needed. They are perfect little child-friendly seats. Hassocks are ideal canvases for me to experiment with;

"Covering a smaller piece like a hassock with a bold and energetic pattern can also add color and life to a room."

stretching one of my fabrics over a hassock allows me to see how a larger piece of furniture might look upholstered with that same fabric.

Decorative pillows are a common, simple way to bring hits of color into a room. My pillows, like my rugs, are rich and pack a good amount of color—they are handmade and embroidered in India. And they take months to create, which I feel makes them precious. These lively pillows look best against solid-colored chairs, sofas, or bedding.

Rugs also make wonderful accent pieces. I love designing rug runners because their oblong shape is the one that as a child I was most inclined to create pattern on. My mother used to cut strips of white cardboard for me to draw or paint on and I would make hundreds of small patterned bookmarks out of them. Who knew that years later I would be designing rug runners whose forms were the same? In my collections for The Rug Company, I have two floral rug runners, Amelie and Bolero. To me they are like large, soft, decorative bookmarks!

Five months after finishing the repeat for my rug Bolero, it arrived from Nepal. We took it home and put it on our living room floor. I could not have imagined the dramatic transformation.

My rugs do not sit quietly on the floor. They make an exuberant statement and do not apologize for being the focal point of the room. Placing solid-colored or white pieces of furniture around colorful rugs will help to balance the look of the room and make it seem less busy.

For those who are hesitant to introduce bold colors in a full-sized rug, a runner is a great, low-impact way to bring color to a space. These long, narrow rugs look terrific in front of a solid, bold piece of furniture.

I also enjoy layering pattern. When I do this, I try to balance the rhythms, colors, and energies of each pattern.

◄ *Begonias*,
acrylic on
canvas

"When I decorate a room and arrange pieces, I try to have an understanding of the dialogue between objects as well as a sensitivity to the balance of color and pattern."

Being that I am a lover of flowers, the majority of my designs are florals. I feel that flowers bring life into a room. When I see a garden or a field of flowers, I take that feeling away with me to the canvas or paper. My desire is not to depict them exactly as they appeared before me, but to translate that feeling into my design. And when I assign names to my products and collections, I love having the freedom to name them in terms of how those flowers make me feel, rather than using the botanical names of the flowers my designs resemble.

Accents are just as expressive and important as larger pieces in a room. They add zest, life, perhaps a dash of something needed to give a space a bit more lift—a hit of vivid color, a contrasting pattern, or a cherished object. Accents can add humor, playfulness, or a welcome bit of dissonance, the way a pinch of spice can spike a savory dish. They are easily movable, and it is one of my favorite games to rotate them from one spot to another or from room to room to see how they affect a different space. In my own home I have beautiful embroidered pillows, handblown glass vases, stools, and throws, all of which add their vitality to the abundance and harmony in our home.

Dinnerware

I remember a trip my parents took to a flea market in a huge barn in the Berkshires when I was very young. They came home with an enormous collection of vintage English dinnerware. What made this collection so extraordinary was that each piece was hand painted in luminous oranges and lime greens, blues and yellows—a truly vivid palette! It was the most beautiful dinnerware collection I had ever seen and it no doubt made a huge impression on my young designer's mind. All the pieces were miraculously in perfect condition. Not one was broken.

To hold any plate or cup from that collection was to hold something truly unique and precious. Each piece was special because it had been painted by hand. So many dinnerware collections you see on the market today take the easy road, repeating the same pattern over and over from plate to teapot, creamer to sugar bowl, with not much thought involved.

When I design dinnerware I use templates, but each bowl, vase, or teapot has its own unique shape for my paintbrushes to dance inside of;

> **"**A collection can also have an eclectic appearance like flea-market finds. A table setting looks interesting and charming to me when dinner plate patterns differ from setting to setting.**"**

I adore cloaking each form in its own design. Rather than repeating the same pattern from one shape to another, I create an individual pattern for each surface. My hope is that I create a special feeling with each piece so a person will want to hold and cherish it.

I adore designing on circular templates. There is something very sensual and feminine about all things round. And I love when a design spills off the edges, leaving half flowers that suggest the continuation of growth. I have always liked the look of a plate fully covered in a design as though a piece of fabric were stretched over its entire surface.

I think a table setting should have a harmonious color scheme. A collection can also have an eclectic appearance like flea-market finds. A table setting looks interesting and charming to me when dinner plate patterns differ from setting to setting. I wanted people to be able to choose from the assortment of patterns I designed, to mix and match as they felt inspired while setting the table. I designed three dinner plates, three salad plates, and various canapés for each collection. Each design has its own individual pattern, but the pieces all share a similar palette.

When I was designing Emma's Garland for Spode, I was inspired to work with a color palette of pink, gold, cranberry, and green that I

felt would create a feeling of springtime. I have always been drawn to rosy tones because they feel warm and embracing.

At home I have a good-sized assortment of vintage English dinner plates that I have collected over the years from flea markets. I am familiar with the beautiful, dainty patterns of the past that are elegant, understated, and timeless. I hoped when designing my collections to create something timeless too, but more exuberant and not so timid. I don't think table settings should be quiet and understated; they should be a joyful part of the celebration.

Naming a collection is a very personal and important part of completing the design process. The name "Emma's Garland" took some time to come up with. After the collection was completed, I started thinking about what to name it. The word "garland" had a musical sound to my ears, and there were clearly garlands around the edge of every bowl and dinner plate. It was a feminine-looking collection and I wanted to give it a name that would reflect that.

One afternoon my husband and I were driving around Washington Square. I was still struggling to come up with the right name for the collection after hours of swishing the word "garland" around in my head. My husband turned to me and asked me to name some of my favorite literary heroines. I looked out over the beautiful brick townhouses lining Washington Square and they conjured up images from Henry James and Jane Austen novels. Suddenly I thought of Emma, one of my favorite Jane Austen heroines. And so the collection became Emma's Garland.

Chicory Hymn was the second collection I designed for Spode. The chicory flower is a light-blue wildflower that is tempting to pluck from the grass but quickly fades once it's been picked. When my husband and I lived in the Catskills, the front of our house faced a huge field of them that gave the impression that a beautiful blue sky had fallen on the field. This memory inspired me to design a pattern that incorporated both the flower's shape and its particular shade of blue.

The word "hymn" means "song in praise of," and I am fond of musical words like "hymn" and "psalm" that allude to the divine. When stringing the two words "chicory" and "hymn" together, I liked the way they united to mean "a song in praise of the chicory flower."

Normally I gravitate toward designing in warmer palettes, but the Chicory Hymn collection was an opportunity for me to create a contrast to the rosy Emma's Garland, and also to explore my new love affair with blues and greens. I was well aware of the importance of blue in the market and its universal appeal, but I couldn't bear turning out another Delft pattern. I mixed a teal blue reminiscent of a William Morris wallpaper pattern I had always admired. I felt the color would pay homage to my love for the Arts and Crafts movement, one of my favorite periods, which sprang from a desire to return to the beauty and integrity of handcrafted design after the Industrial Revolution.

My dinnerware collections have been described as modern Arts and Crafts and I am happy they evoke such an association. I have always loved the look of handcrafted objects and prefer to see a human touch in design. I think it adds warmth and a sense of preciousness because it connects others to the intimacy of the artist's creative process.

I was asked in a recent interview for *Food & Wine* magazine if, when I design dinnerware, I considered how food would look on it. This was a question I had not been asked before and I replied, "Truthfully, no. I was more concerned with creating a beautiful looking table. I wasn't thinking at all about how food would look on the pieces I designed."

Part of the fun I have when designing dinnerware or other accent pieces is that I don't concern myself with how food will look on a plate or how my design will translate to a rug lying on the floor. It's wonderful to have that element of surprise left in the creative process. My top priority is to create something I feel is beautiful, rather than to manipulate a design to meet industry standards and expectations.

The first time I saw food on the dinnerware pieces I had designed was when Spode sent me professional photographs they had taken of my collections that they intended to run as ads. These photos were tastefully styled and it was not until that moment that I saw how beautiful the food looked on them. I was delighted. I had managed to create two joyful collections of contrasting color and pattern ready to celebrate any occasion!

Abstract Gardens

The first canvases I ever painted were extremely free and abstract. When I look at them now, I am not sure they came from my brushes. I think in the beginning stages of working with a new medium the territory is so vast and our desire to explore so intoxicating that we are lifted out of consciousness.

I remember viewing an impressive exhibit of abstract charcoal drawings in a gallery on Broome Street back in the days when SoHo was the gallery mecca of New York City. Being a color addict I was never really drawn to black-and-white compositions. This artist, however, handled the medium in a way I had never seen before. His work was full of fiery energy and was exciting to look at.

A few weeks later I mustered my confidence and took a few of my paintings to the gallery to see what sort of response I would get. I was informed that the gallery only viewed slides twice a year. However, the young man who managed the gallery saw that I had

◀◀ *Urban Garden,*
acrylic on canvas

the paintings in the back seat of our car and good-naturedly offered to look at my work. The next thing I knew, the gallery owner walked into the room and asked if I had more paintings like those. That day I was offered my first SoHo gallery one-woman show.

Inferno, ▶
acrylic on canvas
Rhapsody, ▶▶
acrylic on canvas

Yellow Hill, ▶
gouache
on paper

◄ *After a Rain*,
acrylic on
canvas

Cherokee Flower, ▶
acrylic on paper

◀ *Dandelions*,
acrylic on paper

Water Lilies, ▶
acrylic on paper

◄ *Marc's Tree*,
acrylic on paper

> " My painted gardens are all symphonic compositions to me. I feel a desire to embrace all voices and tonalities with a sensitivity to harmony and dissonance, giving each voice and each color its moment to sing. "

Opening night was magical. All of the paintings were splendidly lit, and I had never witnessed my work in this way before. Broome Street was abuzz with gallery hoppers beneath a full moon. I sold a few paintings and the show stayed up for a month.

For a little while longer I painted abstract landscapes, but gradually my canvases moved toward total abstraction with almost no reference to nature. About two years later I took a break from painting large-scale canvases and started focusing on painting textiles. It was time to get back to working in textile design, so I started assembling my portfolio in hopes of selling my prints on my own to the fashion industry.

After devoting a few years to painting thousands of silk and paper textile designs, I started feeling the desire to return to canvas. It was interesting to move back onto a large surface again, and I discovered that I no longer had a desire to work in abstracts. Instead, I wanted to paint large gardens. This was a new direction and it excited me to paint flowers on such a large scale, which made them seem even more bold and dynamic. I had been painting them so intimately on silk and paper for years, but with gouache and dyes, not with acrylic. It was like learning a new language.

Maggie's Garden, ▶▶
acrylic on canvas

*Tuscan
Garden,* ▶
acrylic on
canvas

◄ *Sienna Garden*, acrylic on canvas

"I think in the beginning stages of working with a new medium the territory is so vast and our desire to explore so intoxicating that we are lifted out of consciousness."

For years I have bounced between my love for painting large gardens and my desire for pure, formless color abstractions. I have always admired the paintings of Abstract Expressionists like de Kooning, Krasner, Pollock, and Kline, and have been equally drawn to great painters of florals—Nolde, Matisse, Jawlensky, Klimt, Münter, and Demuth. I also admire the work of Hans Hofmann, the man considered the greatest twentieth-century teacher of painting. The freedom to move away from form, to pare down to the raw essence of something, is refreshing and challenging to me.

Since I was a little girl, painting has always brought me pleasure. There were no critical voices in that sacred space. To later be given validation and support for something I had nurtured on my own was extremely meaningful to me. And although I have always fantasized about having a teacher to look up to, like a Matisse, a Hofmann, or an Albers, I question whether I truly would have wanted such a relationship.

The liberty I have always had to express my love for color and to fly freely with my ideas allowed me to move through the different phases and styles without judgment. There were no parameters, no rules, and no teachers to please.

◄◄ *Garden of Hope*, acrylic and oil on canvas

Garden with ▶
Blue Tulip, acrylic
on canvas

◄ *Turquoise Garden*, acrylic on canvas

*Color Essay
with Peach*, ▶
acrylic on
canvas

◄ *Color Essay with Turquoise*, acrylic on canvas

" For years I have bounced between my love for painting large gardens and my desire for pure, formless abstractions. The freedom to move away from form, to pare down to the raw essence of something, is refreshing and challenging to me. "

The work in this chapter gives a visual tour of the journey I took on canvas from 1993 to the present. The pieces titled "Color Essays" are about my love for using pure color free from form. In these I am alone with color—face to face with its pure essence. In them, color is not disguised or supported by form and has only its relationship to itself and the adjacent hues. I see these works as color meditations because their color frequencies seem to vibrate off the canvas. These canvases are gardens to me too, but their leaves, flower heads, and stems have been taken out of focus so they are softened and quieted.

◄◄ *Color Essay with Green,* acrylic on canvas

Design Philosophy

I have become increasingly aware of a trend, not only in my own industry but in others as well, that things made by hand with real craftsmanship are swiftly becoming a thing of the past. Sadly it appears that we are being seduced by the same new technologies that are saturating our daily lives, removing us from the importance of eye contact and touch. Things made by hand and with heart—things that possess integrity and require time, thought, and love to create—are disappearing. On a larger scale, irreplaceable classic architecture is being thoughtlessly torn down, and tall buildings with no attention to character and detail are being swiftly erected in their places.

In my own industry I became aware that my approach to creating textiles by hand was also becoming an anachronism. I had been asked many times by employers to sit in front of a computer screen and design, but I declined. I knew very well what this would be compromising. I could not put a price tag on my love for swishing pigment around on a palette to mix my colors, or on the sensuality

that could only occur with a paintbrush in hand and not a mouse. Whatever accidents occur when I paint I leave in, and adore them all. I enjoy being questioned by people who see where a color bled in a silk textile and ask, "How come you left that in?", while others understand and embrace human imperfection.

My floral textiles and canvases have often been described as organic. One of the reasons I think my work has this quality is because I never think or paint in repeat. Painting in repeat means that the pattern has a mathematical symmetry, motifs reappear in perfect echo and alignment at certain points in the design. Whenever I see textile

"Whether I'm designing a dinner plate or a rug, I never plan a single motif or pattern before I begin painting. Working in this manner is much like improvisation in music."

detail from
textile design, ▶
acrylic on
canvas

designs that are extremely symmetrical, I am a little bored by them. They lack the unpredictability you find in nature—in life!

Whether I'm designing a dinner plate or a rug, I never plan a single motif or pattern before I begin painting. Working in this manner is much like improvisation in music. It is both exciting and liberating to leap onto a clean white surface of paper, canvas, or silk and dance upon it with my brush. I feel that patterns remain fresh to the viewer's eye for a longer period when they are created in this way. I have never been interested in manipulating a design to meet industry trends or expectations. I was always amused by how few risks were taken in fashion studios and how closely people adhered to trend reports. The sheep's outfit never felt comfortable for me; my heart and hand needed to fly freely, like a goat in a Chagall painting.

Creating something beautiful is and always will be my main objective. Harmony and joy are key elements in my work and I express them through vivid color and exuberant motifs. My philosophy is simply to create interior spaces that are healing gardens. Imagine how it might feel to stand amid a field of poppies or jewel-like wildflowers! That is the joyful sensation I wish to bring into the home, an interior garden for all seasons.

resources

C Y UPHOLSTERY
Charles Young
208 East 7th Street
New York, New York 10009
212-473-7088

EDITIONS LIMITED
4090 Halleck Street
Emeryville, California 94608
800-228-0928
510-923-9770
www.editionslimited.com

GALISON
28 West 44th Street
New York, New York 10036
212-354-8840
www.galison.com

KOEHLER PHOTOGRAPHY
Gene Koehler, photographer
Trish Koehler, stylist
1044 Industrial Drive, Unit 19
West Berlin, New Jersey 08091
856-767-4422

MICHAEL ANCHIN GLASS COMPANY
51 South 1st Street
Brooklyn, New York 11211
212-925-1470
www.michaelanchin.com

THE RUG COMPANY
88 Wooster Street
New York, New York 10012
212-274-0444
www.therugcompany.info

All rugs in this book are from
the Kim Parker Home collection
for The Rug Company.

SHAH RUG INTERNATIONAL
Yousuf Shah
Firdousabad, Batamaloo
Srinagar, Kashmir, India
91-194-451437
shahrug@vsnl.com

SPODE
(owned by The Royal China
& Porcelain Companies, Inc.)
1265 Glen Avenue
Moorestown, New Jersey 08057
856-866-2900
www.spode.co.uk

All dinnerware and giftware
images in this book are part of
the Kim Parker Home collection
for Spode.

All decorative pillows in this book
are from the Kim Parker Home
collection, www.kimparker.tv

Lush Garden, ▶
acrylic on
canvas